The People

VS

The Elite

A Manifesto for Democratic Revolution
Or,
Survival in the 21st Century & Beyond

J. Todd Ring

A portion of the royalties from this book will be donated to the David Suzuki Foundation
and to Ecojustice for their important work in defending the future of us all.

"I have sworn upon the altar of God eternal hostility against every form of tyranny over the mind of man."

– Thomas Jefferson

*"I hope we shall crush in its birth
the aristocracy of our monied corporations
which dare already to challenge our government
to a trial by strength,
and bid defiance to the laws of our country."*

— Thomas Jefferson, 1812

"Turning and turning in the widening gyre
The falcon cannot hear the falconer;
Things fall apart; the centre cannot hold...
The best lack all conviction, while the worst
Are full of passionate intensity."

– T.S. Eliot, The Second Coming

Ozymandias

I met a traveller from an antique land
Who said: "Two vast and trunkless legs of stone
Stand in the desert . . . Near them, on the sand,
Half sunk, a shattered visage lies, whose frown,
And wrinkled lip, and sneer of cold command,
Tell that its sculptor well those passions read
Which yet survive, stamped on these lifeless things,
The hand that mocked them, and the heart that fed:
And on the pedestal these words appear:
'My name is Ozymandias, king of kings:
Look on my works, ye Mighty, and despair!'
Nothing beside remains. Round the decay
Of that colossal wreck, boundless and bare
The lone and level sands stretch far away."

– Percy Bysshe Shelley

A Farewell to Kings

When they turn the pages of history
When these days have passed long ago
Will they read of us with sadness
For the seeds that we let grow?
We turned our gaze
From the castles in the distance
Eyes cast down
On the path of least resistance

Cities full of hatred, fear and lies
Withered hearts and cruel, tormented eyes
Scheming demons dressed in kingly guise
Beating down the multitude and
Scoffing at the wise

The hypocrites are slandering
The sacred Halls of Truth
Ancient nobles showering
Their bitterness on youth
Can't we find the minds that made us strong?
Can't we learn to feel what's right
And what's wrong?
What's wrong?

Cities full of hatred, fear and lies
Withered hearts and cruel, tormented eyes
Scheming demons dressed in kingly guise
Beating down the multitude and
Scoffing at the wise
Can't we raise our eyes and make a start?
Can't we find the minds to lead us
Closer to the heart?

– Lee, Peart, Lifeson

"Our strategy should be not only to confront empire,
but to lay siege to it.
To deprive it of oxygen.
With our art, our music, our literature, our stubbornness,
our joy, our brilliance, our sheer relentlessness"
...
"Another world is not only possible - it is already being born.
On a quiet day, I can hear her breathe."

– Arundhati Roy

Table of Contents

Preface
&
Acknowledgements

*T*here are those who watch history unfold; and there are those who are clueless, until history hits them over the head, because they have been lost in a fantasy world of propaganda, consumerism, escapism, scapegoating, entertainment addiction and distraction; and then there are those who shape it.

It is in times like these that we need more of the latter – the active ones, and not the mere spectators – and you, dear reader, and all of us, should want to be among the latter as well.

As Virgil said, *"Fortune favours the bold."*

Or as Helen Keller said, *"Life is a daring adventure, or nothing."*

And yet, as T.S. Eliot put it *"The best lack all conviction, while the worst are full of passionate intensity."*

It is true, as the Hopi prophecies state: *"When the people become wooden, a great calamity will befall them."* The problem is not in human nature, nor even in a ruling elite: but with a learned helplessness among the masses, and a woodenness, and a weak-kneed servility, which stems from it. It is not that the people are too bold. It is that they *lack* boldness. This must be rectified, and immediately, or we are in truly dire straits.

There is a great deal of confusion in the world; and yet, as Noam

1

Chomsky has rightly said, many times, the great majority of people have a pretty good idea of what is going on, what is wrong, and what they want. And furthermore, *"The great majority of people have basically decent impulses."*

The problem, as I have argued before, is not ignorance, nor human nature, but a learned helplessness, a pervasive illusion of powerlessness; and the apathy and denial and avoidance of reality, and the escapism and voyeurism and vicarious living, the consumerism, and the digital addiction to virtual living, which stem from these roots.

What the people need is an injection of courage, confidence, trust in themselves, inspiration, empowerment – or simple boldness. This is what is needed if we are to stave off or avert the worst of calamities. And we need it now.

The people need to rip the opium and cyanide drip from their arm – which is network "news," the newspapers, television and "social media" – and get back to reality; and maybe even discuss what is really going on, with other people, face to face, and what we should do about it. Then only, can we, the people, become empowered enough, or even clear-minded enough, to take the kind of serious action which is urgently needed if we are going to have any kind of decent future on this planet.

The barbarians are indeed at the gate. In fact, the barbarians have taken over the reigns of power. The barbarians, as we can see by their actions, are the ruling elite themselves. What we must be concerned with, above all, is not a few thugs in far away places, or even the petty thugs on our own streets - but the big criminals, the real criminals, who sit in the capital buildings, and more so, in the financial districts, and who now rule the world.

*

Here are two short passages from a single issue of a serious journal (serious journalism being extremely rare now) that clearly express what is wrong with the world, and clearly imply the solutions to our current problems. The journal is exceptional, but the level of awareness expressed here by readers' letters, is not; even though the eloquence may be.

"When men were ruled by kings, the kings and their church connived to convince the masses that God had chosen their king and that if the king were bad it was the fault of the people and their wicked ways. Today the banksters have replaced the king and have so cowed our political leaders into believing the end of civilization would be hastened by giving the people what they want if it diminished the bankster power, that they effectively rule the world. Deficit spending has come to replace fornication as the deadliest of all sins, to be avoided at all costs."
– Rich Domingue

"The GAO [US General Accounting Office] reports that the US will spend nearly $500 billion in the next decade modernizing its nuclear arsenal. This reminds me of the line from Orwell about destroying the social surplus on useless weaponry so the peony doesn't go to the masses, with the unfortunate consequence of raising their morale and giving them hope of overthrowing their rulers. The ruling class has always preferred corporate welfare, military Keynesianism and Pentagon capitalism over welfare spending for the poor, more or less for that reason." – Ben Debney

Well said, on both counts – and these two short passages get right to the heart of the matter.

The facts, as the Davos Report by Oxfam lays bare, are these:

- The richest 26 individuals now control more wealth than the poorest half of the world's population, down from 68 just three years ago.

- The poorest half of the world's population lost over a trillion dollars in wealth over the past few years alone.

This wealth didn't evaporate, or drift off into space, of course – it was siphoned off by the richest 1%, who are busily taking over the entire planet, and all of the wealth, resources and power on Earth.

Recently Forbes announced that the richest three men in the US – Jeff Bezos, Warren Buffet and Bill Gates – now control as much wealth as the poorest 50% of Americans. And their pieces of the pie are growing, while that of the 99% is shrinking.

This is neo-feudalism. Is this not by now self-evident?

Just 1% of the wealth "owned" by Jeff Bezos (who owns Amazon and the once-respectable *Washington Post*) is equal to the entire health budget of Ethiopia, according to Oxfam.

As the eminent Canadian philosopher John McMurtry has said, in plain and simple language, the richest few are devouring the poor, the middle class and the planet. Clearly, if this is not stopped, things will get far worse than they already are.

It is a feeding frenzy of the rich – and we, the people, and the planet, and all life on it, are the food. Unless and until we change it.

As another venerable Canadian philosopher, John Ralston Saul has said, the billionaire class, and their annual gatherings at places like the World Economic Forum in Davos, Switzerland, form what he called "the new royal court," "the new Palace of Versailles."

Even the leading business journal in the Western hemisphere, the *Financial Times*, admits that Davos and its billionaire patrons have become "the de facto world government."

When do we say, "Enough!"?

When is extreme wealth, and extreme power, simply too much concentrated wealth, or concentrated power, in anyone's hands?

I think we had best reach that conclusion very soon – that we have by now, and in fact, quite long ago, crossed that boundary of allowing too much concentration of wealth and power, and far too much inequality in society. If we do not soon come to that realization, we will be worse than serfs and peasants, as we are now: we will be slaves – and slaves watching the world die around us, at that.

Even the International Monetary Fund (IMF) has recently conceded that corporate-driven globalization, or neoliberalism, doesn't work: it is greatly increasing inequality, not lifting all boats.

It is a trickle-on reality, which underlies the trickle-down theory of neoliberal corporate policies. But even that is euphemistic and understated. It is rape and pillage, pure and simple. It is mass looting.

Further, as the IMF has recently revealed in a study, government subsidies to Big Oil and the fossil fuel industry alone – who have ruled over the US, Canada and much of the world for decades – now total $5 trillion a year globally. That's $5,000 billion a year in subsidies – just to Big Oil and the fossil fuel industry.

We're funding them with $5 trillion a year – so that they can kill us faster with climate change, resource wars and smog. Makes perfect sense – if you're a sociopath, or otherwise insane.

$5 trillion a year. Or roughly 6.5% of global GDP. Think about that. But there is no money for full funding of universal health care, education, pensions, green energy, a real jobs program, childcare, pharma care, affordable housing, or even fixing the roads and bridges and crumbling infrastructure.

Nope, Big Oil and Big Coal need it all, folks. So just suck it up, along with all the lies and smog you're sucking up, and watch the world die: because this is just the way it has to be.

Note also that according to international development organizations, global poverty could be eliminated at a cost of less than a trillion dollars – that's one-fifth of what we are giving away every year to Big Oil and the fossil fuel industry in annual global subsidies.

The cost of Arnie's hydrogen highway in California was $100 million. $1 trillion, which is 10,000 times that amount, would be more than enough to build a hydrogen fuel infrastructure, with full wind and solar power to generate the hydrogen fuel, for the entire continent of North America. And that is just one-fifth of the money we are giving away globally to Big Oil every year.

Add another $4 trillion, and we could convert every single fossil fuel-burning automobile in the world to run on clean, zero-emission, renewable solar hydrogen fuel. (We can't wait for electric replacement vehicles: not while we have a billion petrol-burning vehicles on the road, obviously. Nor do we have the rare Earth metals for the batteries, even if we could wait another 20 years to replace the existing global fleet, which we clearly cannot.) And that's just the equivalent of one year's global subsidies to Big Oil.

The cost of a high-speed train from Montreal to Windsor, and connecting Ottawa and Toronto, has been estimated at $30 million. We give away, at present, $20 billion in subsidies to Big Oil in Canada, or 60 times that amount, *every year*.

With $1 trillion we could build a high-speed rail system for the entire North American continent – and still be using just one-fifth of what we are currently giving away in direct subsidies to Big Oil and the fossil fuel industry globally, every single year.

How much clearer can it be that we are being lied to: that there is no lack of money – that we are being systematically robbed, and robbed blind?

"Austerity" is a lie. Neo-liberalism is a pack of lies. Corporate globalization is built on a mountain of lies.

The ruling elite and their minions in political office, academia, and the media, are systematically lying to the people – and probably to themselves as well, because they truly do seem to be just that insane.

We can add to this grand theft, or mass looting of the people and the planet for the benefit of the super-rich and the corporate empire they control, the more than $2 trillion spent on war and militarism annually – and on their bedfellow, which is the growing police state.

Note also that there is an estimated $11 to $20 trillion hidden in the secret offshore bank accounts of the super-rich. (The Panama Papers, among other sources, give us some good indications.) Along with the trillions of dollars in yearly tax breaks (public give-aways) and subsidies (more public give-aways) to the largest corporations and the super-rich who control them, there is this vast pool of (largely unethically gained, or at least obscenely unethically horded) wealth which could be put to better uses than $100 million private yachts. Taxing just 50% of it for use directed toward the common good, to heal the planet and abolish poverty, for example, would take us a giant step toward a much better, cleaner, more peaceful, truly sustainable and livable world.

I would recommend a 90% tax on all personal wealth over $10 million, as well as a 90% tax on all personal income over $1 million a year, and all corporate profits over $1 billion a year; but any serious proposal with some guts, would be good start, and a refreshing change from the looting and pillaging model we now subscribe to.

Leave family farms alone; and leave small business alone – they are the engine of the economy, as well as the primary employer. We would be unwise in the extreme to place an excessively heavy burden on either of them, as we are doing now – and in severe and extreme ways. What we would be wise to do, would be to subsidize small farms, co-ops, small businesses and start-ups – not squeeze them to their limits, and more often out of existence, as we are now doing.

But should we tax the richest 1% and the largest, most profitable corporations? Even more importantly, most essentially and most urgently, should we rein in, dethrone and remove from power the super-rich plutocrats, the oligarchs who have effectively taken over most of the nations and the greater part of the world? Of course we should, and must. If we have any remaining common sense, or any sanity, we will do both – and immediately, without hesitation.

What is clear, and undeniable, is that we have to start somewhere – and now. The present system is gutting both the people and the planet; and it neither can continue, nor will continue, for long.

Mark my words. Either revolution or collapse will bring this system to a halt, and soon – replacing it either with something better; or, if we are too timid, with the collapse of our civilization.

In short, the ruling policy of globalization and neoliberalism, which is the ruling ideology of the world today, is this: austerity for the people; and a giant feeding trough for the large corporations and the richest few who control them; and along with a welfare state for the rich, a global propaganda and entertainment-distraction industry, a police state, and a heavily armed global military and financial empire to keep the people obedient, meek, shell-shocked, disempowered, distracted and divided – all to ensure that the new global neo-feudal corporate oligarchy remains unchallenged while it rapes and pillages the people and the planet.

There is no shortage of money. The rich are awash in money. We're squandering more than seven trillion dollars a year on subsidies to Big Oil, the police state and the war machine, alone – to mention only three of the black holes that are swallowing up the people's wealth and their power.

What we have is mass looting on a grand scale. What we need is a redirection of this massive amount of money and resources, which currently goes into feeding war and militarism, neo-fascism, neo-feudalism and fossil fuel addiction, and the profits and privilege of the few, at the growing expense of the people and the Earth.

Instead of funding accelerating inequality, neo-feudalism, crypto-fascism and a police state, war and militarism and war-profiteering, Big Oil and our suicidal addiction to fossil fuels, ever bigger bail-outs and subsidies for the big banks, the financial elite and the largest corporations, and a feeding frenzy of the super-rich upon the great majority of the people and the planet; why not redirect and channel this multi-trillion dollar a year fund into helping people and the planet?

The political and business elite, and their whores in the corporate and state media (pardon my frank language, but these are the plain facts of the matter) are lying to us, while they continue looting the planet and destroying all that remains of democracy, liberty, human rights and civil liberties, constitutional rule, and any chance of a decent future on Earth.

We do not have to accept the dark, dystopian path we are being led, or more accurately, driven and corralled down. We can change this. Money is not the issue or the problem. There is no lack of money. It is simply being squandered and stolen, en masse.

Lack of popular will, inspiration, empowerment, vision, imagination, courage, boldness, or spine, is the only real issue. We must simply stand up.

This is not complicated to understand. This is not advanced physics. These are simple power dynamics, that an intelligent six-year-old child could understand.

The majority of the people understand it well enough, in broad strokes. What is lacking, however, is inspiration, empowerment, confidence, solidarity, and simple boldness.

Well, it is now or never.

*

The idea of a Green New Deal, as simply a starting point of reference, and nothing more – that is, a comprehensive and bold, public infrastructure-building project, designed to lay the foundations for a truly green and sustainable society for the 21st century and beyond, that will simultaneously employ millions of people and kick-start the economy out of the global recession and stagnation it has been in since the crash of 2007/2008 (which, by the way, I predicted, when virtually everyone was saying things are just rosy, and are going to stay that way) – is an idea that is now beginning to be discussed more widely.

Such a plan, which I outlined in detail in my 2014 book, *Enlightened Democracy: Visions For A New Millennium,* is not surprisingly being attacked and dismissed by establishment figures and the corporate and state media (there is little difference between the two, now that they have merged) as "too controversial," or simply as, "politically impossible." The reality of our situation, however, is quite the opposite.

The reality, in the early days of the 21st century (the beginning of the sixth millennium in our experiment in "civilization"), is that a Green New Deal is an extremely *moderate beginning* to the kinds of changes which are urgently needed, and which cannot be delayed, without truly grave results ensuing from our refusal to act, our reticence, our avoidance and evasion and denial of reality, and our neglect.

It is too little boldness and action, not too much of it, which is our greatest danger now. The Titanic sinks, while the ruling elite sip brandy, champagne, scotch and wine, and debate the placement of the deck chairs – or the colour and design of fabric prints for the deck chairs. This will not do – not for the sane, at least.

The reality of our situation is that we either make some very bold changes now – not in six months, or six years, or some decades ahead, but now – in order to address the twin crises of our civilization, which are: staggeringly great and exponentially growing inequality of wealth and power, on the one hand; and a rapidly growing and accelerating ecological crisis on the other – or our society will either explode into violence and civil war, or implode under the weight of an ecological crisis that was essentially disregarded and brushed aside, until it was too late, and the house of cards which is our civilization, begins to collapse – or both.

It is denial and avoidance that are now our greatest dangers. We should be perfectly clear about that. We either deal with reality, or reality will deal with us. There is no third option in the political economics of the real world.

At present, our society continues to live inside a bubble of denial. That bubble is about to rupture. Either it will rupture through non-violent revolution, or it will rupture through violent upheaval – or it will simply burst and implode, due to a prolonged and stubborn policy of ecological neglect and malfeasance. What I am arguing for here, is the least dangerous of the three options: non-violent revolution.

I think of something that John F. Kennedy said, which is as relevant and as prescient today as it was when he made the statement: *"Those who make peaceful revolution impossible will make violent revolution inevitable."*

Yet the reality today is even more stark: if we prevent peaceful revolution, or simply do not support it strongly enough to ensure that it happens, then we will not only have violent upheaval and civil war - we will also have the beginnings of a full-scale ecological collapse.

Calm, reasoned thought and action, therefore, are now on the side of revolution. The alternative is simply a cataclysm – and one of our own making.

*

"If you are afraid of writing something that might offend someone, why write anything at all?"
– Thomas Merton

I think about some of the truth-tellers that I have loved the most: Martin Luther King Jr., Gandhi, Thoreau, Emerson, Einstein, Twain, Chomsky, Bookchin, Kropotkin, Bertrand Russell, Emma Goldman, Aldous Huxley, George Orwell, Alan Watts, Erich Fromm, Peter Dale Scott, Nafeez Ahmed, Ken Wilber, Joanna Macy, Rianne Eisler, Helena Norberg-Hodge, Arundhati Roy, Vandana Shiva, Ronald Wright and David Suzuki, Thomas Merton, Joseph Campbell and Allan Wallace, Thomas Jefferson and Thomas Paine, Charles Dickens, TS Eliot, Yeats and Blake, to name just a few, and to omit a great many.

(I have deliberately not included footnotes or formal academic references, because while this book is both scholarly and extremely well researched, I would say, and based upon quite literally tens of thousands of hours of reading, reflection and study; I did not want to scare people off. Many people are frightened away by books that look too academic, though they should not be. I did not want to talk solely to the academics, to the ivory tower, but to the people broadly; and so, I spoke in a very conversational and informal manner in the writing, so as to include, and make accessible to, the widest possible audience. But this is a very incomplete bibliography and list of references for anyone who wants it.)

Their writing, the writing and speeches of the truth-tellers I most dearly love, tends to be very plain-spoken; and is at times, both fierce and frank, and unapologetically so – as, I think, all good writing, or at least all good political or philosophical writing, can and must be. There is no squeamishness about their writing or manner of speech. They are not afraid of themselves, of the subject matter, of the truth, or of what anyone might think. They simply speak the truth as they see it, to the best of their very human understanding, which is all that anyone can do, without compromise and without fear.

At this time in our human history, nothing less will do. So, you have my apologies in advance for an, at times, blisteringly honest account of what I see as the truth of the matter. I make no apologies, other than for the inevitable errors, for which I take full responsibility, and hope are few. The truth will speak for itself. Hopefully I have done it some justice; and I believe I have. But let that be, of course, for the reader to decide.

My debt of gratitude is great, and there are far too many people, living and dead, known to me directly, and more often, known to me only by their words, or their art, or their acts, to possibly list here. My family and friends, of course, and many mentors, I must thank deeply and sincerely, including the most venerable Lama Zopa, Lama Tharchin, Kirti Sendrag Rinpoche, and professor emeritus of philosophy at Trent University, Robert Carter, whose world-class scholarship and brilliance were matched only by his kindness and utter approachability.

For all the patience I have been shown, which was sometimes great, and for all the kindness I have been graced to receive, and for all the knowledge and understanding which I was bequeathed, and which I hope to have, not only transmitted without too many errors, but synthesized, and perhaps at times, distilled, I cannot express enough thanks. My bucket was, most extremely fortunately, emptied – with a gaping hole, and the bottom dropped out – and filled anew. Thank you, my teachers and mentors, family and friends, for a kindness that is too great for words.

May these words inspire action – and action filled with love.

JTR,
March 11, 2019

A Just Society,
or a Dead World:
Our Choices Have Narrowed to Two

*T*here are a few nations in the world where things are in a fairly positive state, or at least moving in a positive direction, in terms of democracy, justice, or the environment. Mexico, after the 2018 election of Lopez Obrador and the new Moreno party; Bolivia, under the leadership of Evo Morales; Iceland and the Nordic countries are among the few. For most of the world, including Britain, Canada, the United States, and most of Europe, the picture does not look so good. For most of the world, revolution is frankly in order, because the democratic system is broken, has been high-jacked and taken over by the international business elite or by some other form of elite rule. And revolution remains, or has become, the only serious option for serious social change – which is clearly, urgently needed, for reasons of social justice, and for reasons of simple survival, due to the obvious and by now undeniable and severe ecological crisis our tiny fragile planet is facing. This is the context that we must understand, or come to understand, and very soon. Or rather, essentially *now*.

Let us begin. Let us begin to unravel the tangled ball of yarn, and come to better understand the mess we're in, so that we can begin to get ourselves out of it.

*

What constitutes a just society? That was the question Plato, the founder, or one of the primary founders, of Western political philosophy asked. The question is still one of the most important that we can and should ask. And by the state of our present society, I would say that we have failed to answer that question adequately, or even earnestly, or honestly, at all.

In my first year of university, in my first course in philosophy, we read just two books – and they were an excellent place to start: Plato's *Republic*, and Descartes', *Meditations on First Philosophy*. My first essay in philosophy was a critique of Plato's political philosophy, and his idea of the just society being one that is based upon a strict caste or class structure and ruled by a benign and wise elite. Plato hated democracy, because the democracy of Athens in ancient Greece had sentenced his beloved teacher, Socrates, to death, for asking too many questions; and worse, for encouraging others, and especially young people, to ask questions. For that, he was sentenced to death, for "corrupting the minds of the youth." Plato found this unforgivable and became a fierce opponent of democracy – and a fierce elitist and authoritarian in response.

My intuitive reaction to Plato's concept of a just society being one that is ruled by a benign, all-powerful, authoritarian elite, was to be deeply skeptical. If it worked, it could be wonderful. But the chances of it working seemed slim to me, and the chances of it working well over the long term seemed remote at best – while the chances that it would simply be another instance of abuse of powers, seemed to me to be very high – far too high to risk. My gut reaction was to mistrust any form of elitism or authoritarianism. More than three decades later, experience and study have only confirmed my initial wariness of great concentrations of power in society, and amply so.

So, my first thoughts in political philosophy, knowing nothing, and having read next to nothing, was to agree with something that Winston Churchill famously said, and which I had not heard at that time, but only encountered later: *"Democracy is the worst form of government possible, except for all the others."*

Since then, I discovered that sensible, thoughtful people as disparate and diverse as Henry David Thoreau, Noam Chomsky and Bertrand Russell in the West, and the Taoist philosophers and sages in the East, agree wholeheartedly with that basic conception, or view, of social and political philosophy: that is, we must guard against excessive concentrations of power, or else suffer the consequences.

Guarding against the abuse of power, and hence, against excessive concentrations of power, was my first and primary instinct, in terms of social or political philosophy. It seems my instincts, so I found out later, were to reaffirm the concerns of people and movements like Thomas Jefferson and the Enlightenment: guard against excessive concentrations of power in society, lest the sop to Cerberus be lost, and tyranny arise – and actively, passionately, and vigilantly promote, protect, advance, and defend, instead, *liberty, equality, and solidarity.*

*

More than three decades and fifty thousand hours of reading, studies, research and reflection later, my initial instincts have only been confirmed – time and time again, with ample and repeated evidence and examples.

The gist of it is this: either we vigilantly guard against excessive concentrations of power, and promote and defend liberty, equality, solidarity and democracy; or we watch the world descend into madness and the evil power games and narcissism of self-proclaimed elites, as they stumble and claw to ever further inflate their sense of (infantile) grandiosity.

Today, it is the same as it was in the pharaohs' time, or the feudal kings and aristocratic lords – in broad strokes, and in essence: one empire has given way to the next; and a long parade of fools has vied for title of sovereign over all. They each stumble and fall in the end, but not before wreaking much havoc, and sowing great suffering upon the minds and bodies of women and men.

We have yet another hierarchical, essentially feudalistic society, run by and for the elite; with much lip service and many fine but hollow words devoted to such things as "freedom," and "democracy" and "human rights." But the world is still ruled by the few, and at the (ever-increasing) expense of the many.

*

This is not to say that there is some secret society in charge. Perhaps there is; I don't know. But I tend to agree with Chomsky on most things, including his statement, that, of course the elite have their clubs – "they're not very interesting." What Chomsky has emphasized, and what I am emphasizing, is the central concept, and fact, of *class*: that is, the question of where power lies, and who holds it.

As Chomsky also noted – again, with his common intelligence and precision of perception, which are at a level that is unfortunately very uncommon – If you want to understand a society you have to look at where power lies. That should be self-evident, a truism.

In our present, early 21st century society, a tiny elite of multi-billionaires and their minions, to be frank about it, rule the world. It is anything but democratic; it is anything but just; and in very important ways, it is anything but free – or even sane.

It is not a change in the faces of power that we need; but a change of systems.

Donald Trump is not the problem. The problem is a system which gives rise to people like Trump – false populists who proclaim themselves the champions of the people, who in reality, are merely falsehoods writ large, and servants of the ruling oligarchy; whether they are intelligent enough to realize it or not – and often they are not.

It is not a change of people in power that is needed, but a change in the structures *of* power, that we need.

We have had a series of neoconservative and neoliberal political "leaders" who have functioned as little more than figureheads for the neo-feudal corporatist state and the ruling corporate oligarchy. We need something more, and better, than this.

I am sure that Donald Trump likes to think of himself as a fine president, and as one of the most important and powerful men in the world. And no doubt, the latter is true, to a very considerable extent. But secretly at least, even he must realize that he is simply taking orders – because it was made clear to him, from day one in the White House, or very soon after.

The generals rule Trump, just as Wall Street rules the generals. The Pentagon is firmly in charge; and the Pentagon serves the empire, which is corporatist to its black heart.

The military-industrial complex has been firmly in power, as Gore Vidal said, since the *National Security Act* was passed in 1947, giving sweeping and unconstitutional powers to the military and intelligence (sic) elite, and to the business elite who in general control them, and give them their marching orders.

Trump is no more an aberration than Nixon, or Reagan, or Obama, or Clinton, or Bush I or II: they all served the military-industrial-security complex, the empire, and the Wall Street elite – particularly Big Oil and the big banks – which have ruled over the United States for a very long time.

If we are serious about social change – about justice, democracy, freedom, civil liberties, constitutional rule, human rights, equality or freedom, or having a planet to live on that supports a decent human life, and is not a toxic wasteland – then we must look beneath the mere surface of things. We must look at the system of oligarchy which has now, after a slow progression, or degeneration, replaced constitutional democracy and the republic.

And we must challenge it.

In short, we either restore and renew democracy and freedom, or we will inherit, and live in, a very dark and toxic, bleak world, run by quite literally crypto-fascist, rabidly anti-democratic, neo-feudal robber barons, and their political hirelings.

The time is now. It's now or never.

*

As Chomsky has also said, "Trump is a distraction" – as I've written since before his election. Let's not lose sight of the forest for the trees. And while I agree that the removal of Trump from power should be swift, we should keep the bigger picture in mind. Rearranging deck chairs on the Titanic is *not* what we urgently need.

A significant portion of the book you are holding deals with US President Donald Trump – or Phrump, as I prefer to call him, since that seems more fitting; and with the wannabe teen pop star, Justin Bieber Trudeau. But these should be taken simply as case studies. It is the underlying structural, systems, or institutional analysis that matters, and will continue to matter and remain relevant, long after these two buffoons are gone from power.

Before Trump came to power as president of the most powerful nation in history, I thought, in the unlikely event that he becomes president, in all likelihood, barring possible extreme actions, he would be simply another bit player in a much larger drama that he scarcely understands. The Deep State would remain in power – which is to say, Wall Street, Big Oil, the Pentagon and the intelligence community, would remain firmly in control.

And so it has.

When Trump, and his little brother in arms, Justin, "The Boy Wonder" Trudeau, are no longer in power, as is soon likely to be the case, one of two things will have almost certainly transpired. Either another figurehead for the new global corporate empire of neo-feudal oligarchy will have taken their place, or a popular revolution will have begun.

For the sake of the Earth and all living beings on it; for the sake of humanity, and especially for the more than three billion children on the planet, who must make a future in this world somehow; and for the sake of liberty and democracy, civil liberties, human rights, constitutional rule, justice and peace, we should pray that it is the latter, and not the former. And we should be making every effort in our power to ensure that revolution, and not a continuation of business as usual, oligarchy and global pillage, is what comes to pass. And we should do so immediately.

What would someone like Thomas Jefferson, Thomas Paine, Gandhi or Martin Luther King Jr. say about the situation we are facing, and the state we are in? I am sure they would say, "What are you waiting for?"

Revolution now.

*

What is the problem with the world? Well, there are a number of them, of course. Among them: racism, sexism, xenophobia, classism, speciesism, colonialism, neocolonialism, imperialism, power games and power lust, and the resulting very serious risk of nuclear war; excessive bureaucratization, over-centralization, and what Aldous Huxley called over-organization; as well as the problems of over-consumption, a fossil fuel-based economy, and elite vested interests who want to keep it that way; sectarianism and fundamentalism of various kinds, including the most dangerous form of them at the present time, which is the economic and ideological fundamentalism of neoliberalism, or global crony capitalism, and the ideology of infinite growth – which, on a finite planet, is obviously a form of madness, as David Suzuki has said.

We must re-define "progress," "development," "the good life," and also growth. We can have limitless, or nearly limitless, growth in culture, knowledge, science, the arts – but we cannot have limitless growth in the production and consumption of material goods on a finite planet. We either redefine these things and re-orient our thinking to better fit with the realities of our existence on Earth, or we shall simply cease to be. The techo-fantasies will not save us. Nor will the bureaucratic fantasies of the technocratic courtesans to state-corporate power. We can improve our quality of life, while learning to live in harmony with the planet, with other species, and with one another; but unending growth in material production and consumption is a daydream that must cease, or else our species will cease to be. This is not a call for Luddism, or primitivism, or regression to an imagined idyllic utopia of stone age living – it is a call for balance, for awareness, for a shift in thinking and priorities. It is a call for basic sanity. And at present, the political elite, the bureaucratic and technocratic elite that serve them, and the business elite who rule over them all, are living – generally speaking – in a dream world. The people must depose and dethrone them, if we are to stand any chance at a viable future at all.

While we have many problems in early 21st century human society, it is the root of these problems that must be uncovered and addressed, or none of our problems will be resolved, but will only continue to worsen. As I wrote in my earlier book, *Enlightened Democracy: Visions For A New Millennium*, the primary roots of our problems in contemporary society are traceable to these major obstacles to peace, justice, liberty, or even to a sane society: corporatism, nihilism, pervasive alienation and division, an epidemic of an illusion of powerlessness, and the underlying illusion of dualism – the illusion, or more accurately, delusion, that nations, groups, people and things are separate and divided, when in fact they are not, and can never be.

But while our problems are many, and their roots are few, there is one thing which is absolutely central to virtually all the major issues and challenges we face: extreme and grossly excessive concentrations of real power in the world.

We have failed to heed the warnings of people like Thomas Jefferson, when he said, more than 200 years ago, *"I hope we shall crush in its birth the aristocracy of our monied corporations which dare already to challenge our government to a trial by strength, and bid defiance to the laws of our country."*

We failed to listen to our more prescient minds, and so, a tiny elite of oligarchs has taken over. We either now remedy our error, and restore democracy and the rule of the people, by the people, for the people, or we allow a few neo-feudal robber barons to continue to rape and pillage the Earth; to continue to undermine and destroy both democracy and freedom, along with all civil liberties, human rights and constitutional rule; and to further concentrate and consolidate all wealth and power globally in their hands – and all of this with accelerating speed, as anyone who is paying attention can see – until our civilization collapses, due either to ecological ruin, or to nuclear holocaust.

In short, it is either a very dark age of plutocratic neo-feudalism ahead, followed by collapse – or we stand up, and make a change of course.

I think the choice, our choice, should be clear.

Stand now.

JTR,
March 6, 2019

Where We Stand

We must now decide where we stand – and stand for it

US President Donald Trump and his junior partner in crime, Canadian Prime Minister Justin Trudeau, once again have shown they are not working for the people, and not serving the interests of the people: they work for and serve the interests of Big Oil, and the big banks that are even more powerful than the big oil companies, and are in neck-deep with the oil companies in their reckless and truly sociopathic razing and pillaging of the Earth.

Washington and its allies are orchestrating a second coup in Venezuela, attempting the overthrow of the democratically elected government, after elections that over 200 international observers unanimously declared were free and fair, and in an electoral system that President Jimmy Carter called "the best I have seen in the world."

Washington and its allies do not fight for peace, for freedom, for democracy, for the people – they are the enemies of all of these, and they care nothing for them: because they are the tools of the global corporate oligarchy.

As we seen over and over again, the political "leaders" of most nations of the world do not work for or serve the people – they serve the ruling elite, the global business elite: the ruling international oligarchy of billionaires and the corporations they control.

It is time for a change. The people have had enough of billionaires and corporations ruling the world. We've seen what they want. They want what Chomsky quotes frequently from Adam Smith, which is "the vile maxim of the masters" – which is, "all for us, nothing for anybody else." And they don't seem to care if they destroy the Earth's fragile ecosystems, the very basis of life on Earth, and our future, in the process.

Something has to change – and now.

The global power elite of billionaires and giant transnational corporations has to be removed from power. That is step one. Until that happens, we will continue to be fighting rear-guard actions, and losing ground: fighting a raging wildfire with garden sprinklers, and running backwards as fast as we can. We can no longer pretend the reality is any different than this. First, we face the truth of where we stand; then we take strong action, bold action, to resolve the problems. That means, above all, removing the power elite from power; and secondly, making bold changes to ensure that no group of individuals or corporations can ever again amass such dangerously, undemocratically, diabolically excessive powers in such few hands.

We have known for a long time, that *"Power corrupts; and absolute power corrupts absolutely."* Now, we must take the necessary measures to end that currently reigning norm, and to restore power to the people, where it belongs.

What next? The US orchestrates a coup in Canada, because the Canadian government is insufficiently compliant in yielding up its oil and other resources to US corporations? Ah, but that is not necessary when we already have a Quisling government in Ottawa that loyally serves Big Oil and US imperial designs. Or we will see the introduction of legislation and architecture in the US that effectively suspends and overrides, and nullifies democracy, civil liberties, freedom and constitutional rule, and secures the ruling elite as the ruling oligarchs in a crypto-fascist, neo-feudal order of elite rule? But then again, we already have that as well, with the Patriot Act, the Military Commissions Act, the NDAA, the CIA, NSA, TSA, DEA, ICE, the militarized police and the Department of Homeland Security.

No matter what we may think of any given government, the act of overthrowing other peoples' governments is an act of aggression: it is a war crime, and a fundamental undermining of freedom and democracy. If we wish for freedom, as we should, and democracy, as we should, then we must respect the sovereignty and independence of other nations, and not meddle in the internal affairs of other nations. We must swear off "regime changes," coups, interventions, even economic extortion through economic embargoes, which only hurt the poorest. If we want freedom, we must respect the freedom of others. If we want democracy, then we must allow other people in other nations to choose their own government – even if we dislike that government.

Governments have been overthrown by the US in Afghanistan, Iraq, Ukraine, Libya and Honduras, to list just a few in recent years, for the control of oil and gas, pipelines, and other resources; for the sake of corporate profits; and at the expense of democracy, freedom, human rights, the environment and human welfare, all of which have been repeatedly discarded and crushed.

Do we truly want to be ruled by a constellation of international organizations – the IMF, World Bank, WTO, BIS, ECB, the Federal Reserve (which is also controlled by international bankers), and the World Economic Forum – organizations that are all effectively ruled by the big transnational corporations, and by the global power elite, the billionaire elite, who in turn control the biggest banks and corporations? Do we want to see regime change after regime change, coup after coup? Do we want the US military and paramilitary and propaganda machine to be the strong arm for global capital, bending the world and the people of the world, to its will, on behalf of its corporate masters in London, New York, Berlin, Paris and Brussels?

Do we truly want a world filled with ever more desperate and dangerous power games, "interventions" and wars?

Where does it end?

It is clear where it ends. It either ends in a global Orwellian state

27

of crypto-fascist, neo-feudal corporate rule – which is our current trajectory – and finally, in one or another ultimate horror, of either nuclear holocaust, or ecological collapse; or else it ends in revolution, and the people's reclaiming of their democracy, and their power.

I think the sane choice should be clear to all – no matter what your political leanings may be.

The time is late. There is no time left for vacillation or hesitation, obfuscation or denial. The people must decide which they want: a global aristocracy of crypto-fascist, neoliberal, neo-feudal rule by a corporate oligarchy which is at war with humanity and the Earth; or true freedom and democracy, justice and peace, and a future for life on Earth.

The time to decide is now.

Remember, he who hesitates is lost – or under the present circumstances, fated to be extinct.

*

What do we do with the deposed and dethroned power elite, once they have been removed from power, as they will be?

The violent and vengeful among us would argue they be hung, or otherwise killed. But of course, this would not be compassionate, and would be a dangerous precedent – violence sows only more violence; and vengeance is never the answer, nor is hate. There is good cause to send them to trial, to have a public trial for crimes against humanity and the Earth – similar to the Nuremburg Trials, which tried a previous generation of fascists and usurpers. But while that might be just, and fully reasonable, would it be best? What we are seeking, is peace, a just society, a free and democratic society, and a truly environmentally sustainable society. Would such trials end up becoming more of a distraction to the urgent tasks we face? I believe so.

I say, strip them of their power, peacefully, and through non-violent means, then leave them to their own devices. If they threaten or harm the public good, the people or the Earth again, then more serious actions may be needed to contain them – such as sending them to Robben Island, for their crimes of enforcing a global economic apartheid, with comfortable, or even luxurious accommodation, but from which there is no leaving, no parole, no escape, and no contact with the outside world of any kind.

Whatever we do, we must do it soon. In fact, we must do it now.

We know what we must do. We must restore power to the people. We must reclaim our democracy and our power, and now.

Let it begin. The healing of our world awaits, and can wait no longer.

JTR,
February 9, 2019

Trump's Great Wall

*(Or, Crazed Clown Posse Attempts to Slow US Collapse –
But Hastens its Fall)*

*T*ravelling in Mexico just two weeks ago – and I was very sad to leave, I should add – I came across a T-shirt in a shop, next to a painting of Pancho Villa, that read, *"Relax, you're on the fun side of Trump's wall."* It made me laugh; and it was also perfect.

Hysteria abounds North of the border, as do Puritanism, consumerism, materialism, voyeurism, vicarious living, TV and social media addiction – and many other addictions – conformism, stress-overload, division, alienation, insecurity, scapegoating and xenophobia.

In Mexico, while there are major problems – unlike the US and Canada, which have no problems of their own, of course – the nation remains, by and large, a hopeful, often jubilant, vibrant, wonderful country. And, after a long line of deeply corrupt governments, Mexico has a new president, who is a true populist-democrat – moderately centre-left, and a close kin to Bernie Sanders, Tommy Douglas and FDR – and the country is looking even better, and more hopeful, perhaps, than at any time since the Mexican Revolution of Zapata and Pancho Villa in 1910. Mexico is having, what seems to me, the beginnings of a rebirth.

Meanwhile, madness and meanness and narrowness of minds persist in El Norte, as big business consolidates its rule, and rolls back all gains made by the people over the past 800 years since the Magna Carta; and while six corporations, along with the tech giants, Facebook, Twitter and the like, increasingly control the public mind and all the "news" they see – leading them further and faster into a deeply Orwellian nightmare of a society.

This is the real-world context of US President Trump's plans for a Great Wall. If we do not understand this, then we have no real perspective, and everything is a wash of grey fog, or smoke and mirrors.

I have refused to step foot in the US since the Patriot Act was passed in 2001 – a literally fascist piece of legislation that was brought in by the Bush-Cheney regime, and was signed by the hallowed, Saint Obama – effectively nullifying the Constitution and Bill of Rights. I love the United States, its lands and its people, but I refuse to go there until the Patriot Act, the Military Commissions Act, the NDAA and various other pieces of fascist-draconian legislation are overturned and abolished, and the Constitution and Bill of Rights are formally reinstated by Congress and the President, with all due national ceremony and seriousness of purpose, commitment and intent.

So, aside from the border towns, which I would never want to go to, and the Mexican people advise against going to, I feel, not only safe in Mexico, but warmly welcomed, and very much at home.

Which side of the wall feels more dangerous and insane to me? There is no slightest hesitation to my answer. The US is in bad shape and getting worse. Mexico is in bad shape, but improving fast; and it still retains a relaxed and genuine friendliness and warmth, and vibrancy, that the US and also Canada once had, but have largely lost, somewhere along the way to the mall, Walmart and the dollar store, en route to "The American Dream."

The third-worldization of the wealthy nations, is how Chomsky described what was happening thirty years ago, as neoliberalism and corporate globalization were just getting rolling: and the trend has only continued, and accelerated. The blame lays at the feet of Wall Street and Bay Street business elites, and their criminal friends among the political elite and the major media – not with immigrants, and not with Mexico, China, Russia, or any other imagined bogey man.

The roots of the problem are at home – and they are staring us in the face. It's called corporatism: the merger of business and the state.

*

What can we say about Trump's Great Wall? Should we laugh, or cry, scream, or shout for joy? I would hope that most people understand that the last option is not the most informed one.

Many things can be said about US President Donald Trump's plans to build a wall between the US and Mexico. It is a giant waste of money, for one. But then, seven billion dollars is a drop in the bucket compared to the obscenely bloated and murderous, disastrous, and economically ruinous and bankrupting military-industrial-security complex and police state budget, which is destroying the nation; putting the Treasury into insolvency; increasing hate, terrorism, violence and instability in the world; further eroding the vanishing credibility and stature of the United States world-wide; and hastening the decline, decay and fall of the US empire – which is the only good thing that can be said about such organized criminal madness.

The building of the wall would have a negative ecological impact, as well. But then, the environmental impact of such a wall is minuscule compared to the world-razing effects of allowing Big Oil to continue to rule the US, as it has done for many decades already.

The building of a wall would, more significantly, cause further divisions, alienation, and hostility and instability, both within the United States, and also internationally – which makes it a terribly self-defeating plan, that is doomed to failure; and worse, doomed to be a solution which causes more damage, suffering and harm than the problems it is supposed to cure.

If anything, the US needs to become less insular, parochial and inward-looking, less paranoid and xenophobic, less culturally arrogant, less domineering, less aggressive and less bellicose and belligerent – not more so; and more friendly, peaceful, cooperative, and yes, compassionate, humane and just – not less so. And the Great Wall of Trump would only lead the United States and its peoples further down the dark path that it is now travelling at break-neck speed, toward either social implosion, or explosion, as tensions mount, and hysteria, paranoia and misdirected rage threaten to tear the country to pieces, and potentially the rest of the world along with it.

A friendly and respectful cultural dialogue, both within the United States, in all its rich and varied, wonderful diversity, and with other nations and peoples around the world, would be the wise path to follow. But Washington and wisdom are two words that have seldom gone together – at least in anyone's minds but the deranged few who either "lead" it, or blindly worship at its clay feet.

The relationship between the US and Mexico could be one of friendship and peace, as it is between the US and its other closest neighbour, Canada. There are problems, and deep, serious problems, and long-standing problems – I can say frankly, as a Canadian, and a neighbour to the world's most powerful nation in history – with US-Canada relations. As it has been said, being the next-door neighbour to the world's biggest nation-state super-power is like sleeping with an elephant. The Mexican people understand this very well. But there is a very real friendship and peace that exists between Canada and the US, and that is a starting point for more just and free, truly democratic relations – and the model can be applied, with some adjustments for the particular needs and offerings of the nation, to US relations with Mexico, as well. Friendly relations with all; entanglements – including interventions – with none, was the US motto for a long time, and it would be wise for the United States to return to such uncommon, common sense.

The question of immigration is at the heart of the matter, of course; and it is a delicate question, to be sure. But we should start any such discussion by remembering that the US, like Canada and Mexico, and all of the Americas, was built by, and often upon, the power and the labour, the skills and knowledge and talents of millions of immigrants. Along with the bounty of the land, and the native first peoples who often sought to guide and to help and befriend the immigrants and the new colonists, America, and the Americas, was built on a literal flood of immigrants. To be paranoid and mistrustful, or worse, hostile and hateful, toward immigrants now, is severely misguided, as well as deeply self-destructive. It is an act of forgetting; of failing to learn from history. And as Goethe said, "He who can't learn from 5,000 years of history is living hand to mouth."

Illegal immigrants, the target of much fear, scapegoating, and vitriol, by and large, simply want to work, and to send money home to help their families. The US agricultural system would virtually collapse without their presence and their hard-working aid, we should remember; and much of the service industry along with it. If the US truly was a just society, it would treat all immigrants, whether they have their "papers" or not, with dignity and with respect. The fact that the richest country on Earth cannot – that is to say, refuses to – provide universal public health care for all; that it has millions of homeless people living on the streets, not far from country clubs and mansions and glass towers of finance and corporate power of vast proportions; that it cannot, or rather, will not, provide a minimum wage that can support a family in dignity and with a decent minimal standard of living; that it allows its veterans and its elderly to live, far too often and too commonly, in poverty and neglect; that it allows schools and hospitals and health clinics, along with its roads and bridges and infrastructure, to crumble and decay; and that it can proudly boast of monuments like the Statue of Liberty, while turning a cold eye on refugees fleeing violence and despair, and while treating its newer immigrants, who work in the fields and the hotels and the private homes of the rich and affluent, like effluent, and like cattle and dogs – while giving $20 trillion to bail out the deeply corrupt banking elite on Wall Street, and spending a trillion dollars a year on war, preparations for war, and the newly created police state – is a sign that something is deeply wrong in America.

Stop funding the empire and the war machine, stop funding the super-rich and the corporate giants, the big banks and Big Oil, with literally trillions of dollars in subsidies, tax breaks and "bail-outs," and there will be more than enough money to balance the budget, and provide for human needs and environmental protection – including just and decent treatment of immigrants.

The economic woes of the shrinking and falling middle class in the United States, and the growing underclass, which they are falling into, are not the fault of Mexico, nor of immigrants. They are the result of forty years of neoliberal class warfare – or crony capitalism, to put it succinctly. The wall, and the popular rage and fear, are all misdirected. And such misdirected anger and misdirected efforts will only cause further problems and pain – not less.

(As an aside, but an important one, we should note that Saint Obama was the deportation king, as well as the smiling face who continued and intensified and further spread the Bush-Cheney imperial wars abroad, and their project of constructing a police state at home – while filling his government with banking elites, granting them permanent immunity from legal prosecution for their crimes of mass fraud and mass theft from the nation, and handing them trillions of dollars from the already insolvent Treasury. So no, Trump is no great aberration, as I have said before. Perspective is critical.)

*

But maybe the central thing that should be said of Trump's Great Wall, is that it has been tried before: and failed. Does anyone remember the Berlin Wall? Who was saddened when that barbaric piece of symbolic architecture, reflecting a world divided and at war, came tumbling down? No one of sound mind cried. It was a joyous, jubilant moment in our very recent history. Yet Trump is determined to repeat the mistakes of history, as if he, and we, have learned nothing from the past.

There was another Great Wall that was built as well.

The Great Wall of China was built to protect the Empire of China from invasion by foreigners. It was built at incredible expense, and with tremendous, and extreme cost in human lives. It was, of course, a massive undertaking, and when it was finished, it was very impressive, and remains so today. But aside from its beauty as an architectural and cultural landmark, which are truly impressive, did it actually work? Did it really protect the Empire? The answer is no. Not long after the Great Wall was built, the empire fell. And ironically, the empire fell, not because it was invaded by a horde of foreigners; but because the construction of the wall had pushed the already internally divided and unstable society to the breaking point, and internal rebellion brought the empire crashing down into a full collapse.

Trump seems not to know his history. He is damned to repeat it, so it seems. And if he does, we should not be surprised if history repeats itself again, and the Great Wall of America becomes the signal bell, sounding the collapse of yet another once great nation.

"If the blind lead the blind, they will all fall in a ditch." So said Shakyamuni Buddha, and another great sage, as well – and we would be wise to heed the words. (Cultish obedience to authority or group-think will not help us, but wise words will.)

*

Fair trade and open borders are what just societies, and sane societies, will seek and embody in the future. How barbaric do we have to become, before we see that this is the only way to live in peace?

And does anyone know or remember that the US-Mexico border was not only undefended, but largely unmarked, and totally open, for the greater part of the history of both nations? It is entirely possible to live without borders, or at least, without paranoia and border guards. We have done it before – and for many generations we did it, and did it well, and in peace.

Are we concerned about drug lords, drug wars, and the violence and crime that comes with them? There is a simple answer to that: disband the CIA – the world's leading trafficker in cocaine and heroin; end the utterly failed and deceitful "War On Drugs"; seriously address violent gangs and organized crime; give the people, and especially the youth, economic options other than crime and drugs; and decriminalize drugs, as they have done in several nations in Europe, where drug use and crime went down after decriminalization.

Are we concerned with crime? Then create a just society that does not worship at the feet of mammon and greed, and foster community-building, tolerance, compassion and respect for diversity and for all; and crime and violence will steeply decline.

(Small towns and cities in my rural home of Ontario, Canada, now are seeing violent crime, coming fast on the heels of crack, cocaine, heroin, opioids and meth arriving – which in turn followed the economic devastation brought about by the North American Free Trade Agreement (NAFTA). If you want peaceful, safe communities, then you must address justice, and create greater equality and opportunity. Otherwise, you are simply wasting your breath and your time, at best; or at worst, and more commonly, your efforts to combat crime and violence are sowing further social disasters: authoritarianism, fascism, and further, deeper alienation, injustice, violence and division.)

Are we concerned with terrorism? Then close the School of the Americas, in Fort Benning, Georgia, which is the world's leading terrorist training centre, and more essentially yet, swear off empire and military or paramilitary, overt or covert "interventions," since Washington, as global polls repeatedly show the people of the world know very well, is the leading terrorist centre in the world.

A few sobering facts pull the rug out from any and every argument made for Trump's Great Wall. Upon reflection on the facts, the great majority of people, who are neither insane nor intractable ideologues or paranoiacs, can see that it was a bad idea from the start.

*

The central issue and fact of immigration, however, is this: if you allow capital to move freely around the world, you must also allow labour – that is, people – to also move freely around the world; as Adam Smith understood very well. If you do not – if you allow capital to move freely, but restrict the flow of people and labour, as our corporate-ruled world insists upon, then not only is that not a free market, not only is it inhumane and unjust, but it will guarantee the ever-increasing exploitation of the great majority of the people by the business elite and the wealthy few – *as we are seeing* – until we live in one great neo-feudal colony, or prison labour camp, or plantation, with the elite owning everything. We are well on our way to that, right now, as we speak. More fences and walls will only speed the process of building a neo-feudal world. Is that what we really want? I think we had better think again.

JTR,
March 6, 2019

Brexit Madness:
Propaganda and Hyperbole

(Note: By the time this is published, in the book version of the essay, the decision over Brexit may well have been made. That does not make it any less relevant: because clarity and perspective will be imperative and fundamental going forward, as they are at any time, and this essay provides some critically important and much-needed perspective on the central problems facing Britain, Europe and the world.)

*T*he media has been screaming that the world will end if Britain really does leave the European Union (the EU). The absurdity of this now-standard narrative should be clear from the outset to anyone of sound mind. But in case it is not, let us say this.

The EU has been taken over by the European Central Bank and the Western banking elite. The EU has proven it is not only an undemocratic organization, but a positively, and rabidly, anti-democratic organization.

To repeat what should be obvious and known to all, but which has been glossed over and completely ignored, the actions of the EU against Greece, and especially Italy, have proved beyond any trace of doubt that the EU is rabidly anti-democratic.

The troika, as they are called, which is now the de facto government of the EU – the European Council (EC), the European Central Bank (ECB) and the International Monetary Fund (IMF) – were not satisfied with a right-wing billionaire as prime minister of Italy. He was not right wing enough, and not compliant enough with the banking elite who now rule over Europe and most of the world. So, they overthrew the democratically elected government of Italy, and installed a government appointed by the troika, composed, not surprisingly, of unelected banking elites, loyal to the EC, the ECB and the IMF, and in complete contempt for both democracy and the people of Italy. That was a coup by Goldman Sachs and the ECB, though it was not recognized by many people as such.

Given these undeniable facts, given that the EU has proven itself to be the enemy of democracy, the EU must be opposed, and all other considerations are flatly irrelevant.

*

Putting the question of Brexit, or a British exit from the EU, into this context, and in light of these most central facts, we should be able to see that whatever the risks of leaving the EU, in terms of possible negative economic effects, for example – which, by the way, are all hyper-inflated, and vastly exaggerated, and largely a lot of hot air and hyperbole – the risks cannot outweigh the value of democracy: if, that is, we value democracy at all.

If you value democracy, you must oppose the EU. If you value democracy and support the EU, then I would say you are living in a dream world.

So, the question is, what is the bigger danger: an exit from the EU, with potential, though far from certain, negative effects; or effective rule by the ECB and the banking elite, and the effective nullification and destruction of sovereignty, democracy and freedom? I think any sane person can answer that question instantly, and without hesitation.

Leaving the EU presents a far lesser risk than remaining subservient to, and subjugated by, the ECB and the banking elite. Leaving the EU will not immediately grant freedom or independence from the banking elite, but it is one step closer to it; while remaining in the EU guarantees that the troika will continue to rule, the ECB, the IMF and the banking elite will continue to rule, and sovereignty, democracy and freedom will all continue to be eviscerated and crushed.

As Public Enemy said, "Don't believe the hype."

*

As an aside, and as a secondary consideration, we can say this about the economic prospects for Britain, either in or out of the EU.

Membership in the EU has not proven to be the holy grail of economic miracles, as it was proclaimed to be. In fact, entrance into the EU has brought nothing but economic stagnation for many nations. Italy, for example, is about to follow the path of Greece, and is in serious trouble economically – Italy, a once-great economic power. For the past decade Italy's economy has been almost completely stagnant – in fact, it now ranks in the bottom three nations for economic stagnation globally. All sing the praises of the EU now.

The central, and fundamental questions of democracy, sovereignty and freedom aside, any perceived or imagined economic benefits that might be derived from membership in the EU are dubious at best – and purely fictional at worst, and in most cases.

By the way, if you want open borders, which is only humane, and just, and in the long-run, most wise, you don't need the failed club that is the European Union in order to do it. You just do it – as a free and sovereign, democratic nation. Membership in a club ruled by Goldman Sachs and the ECB is not going to promote justice, freedom, or any humanitarian causes, I can assure you. Big Brother allegiances, here as elsewhere, are dangerously misguided.

Furthermore, to conflate concerns over sovereignty and democracy with xenophobia and racism, is also dangerous, and is either a case of misinformation or deceit. There are many people who oppose the over-centralization of powers, because such moves are always contrary to the spirit of democracy and freedom, who are not xenophobic, much less racist, but are simply alert. We should pray we have more of them. Their paucity of numbers puts us all in great danger.

Secondly, if any negative economic fallout does happen in a serious or major way as a result of Britain leaving the EU – beyond the market correction for the ill-advised speculation and wide-spread gambling on the part of investors (speculators) that Britain would vote to remain in – it will most likely be the result of the Western elite punishing the people of Britain for their defiance of the troika and the ruling banking cabal, and seeking a path to greater independence. This cannot be avoided. More importantly, it is part of the price of freedom and democracy, and economic prosperity in the long term.

Thirdly, and most important, in terms of economic considerations at least, Britain's economic woes are exactly the same as those shared by virtually every other Western nation: namely, they are the result of neoliberal policies of corporate globalization. Remaining in or leaving the EU has absolutely nothing to do with it. It is neoliberalism and corporate globalization which are the roots of the problem, both in terms of democracy, and also in terms of simple economics.

*

Look at the numbers.

Since the economic crash of 2007–2008, 95% of the new wealth created has gone to the richest 1%.

The trillions of dollars in "stimulus" programs and bail-outs, which in reality represent a mass theft, and one of the greatest transfers of wealth from the people to the elite in history, has done nothing but line the pockets of the already astronomically rich – mainly the banking elite and their cronies.

In the US, $20 trillion was handed over to the Wall Street banking elite, from the US Treasury and the people of the United States. All that it has bought is further consolidation of wealth and power for the ruling banking elite and their friends – exactly as it was meant to. Has it "trickled down" to Main Street and the people? No, they have been *trickled on*.

A recent systems analysis from Switzerland confirmed the obvious: a small group of large corporations – roughly 40, mainly banks – effectively control the global economy.

A recent study from Princeton also confirms the obvious: the US is no longer a democracy, but an oligarchy, and the bottom 99% of the population have little to no influence on public policy – exactly as with Britain, the EU, and most nations of the world, where transnational corporate powers have effectively taken over the nation-states, and have usurped and eviscerated both freedom and democracy.

And a report released by Oxfam this year confirms that neoliberalism and corporate globalization has failed utterly in its stated aims of lifting all boats, benefiting all people, and reducing poverty, as even the IMF now admits. The report shows that the poorest half of humanity lost nearly half its wealth in the past few years alone – to the richest 1%, who now control 99% of the wealth of the planet; while the richest 68 people on Earth now control as much wealth as the poorest half.

Let those numbers sink in.

We are being driven at break-neck speed, by corporate globalization and neoliberalism – or class warfare waged by the super-rich upon the rest of us, to put it more directly – into a global neo-feudal order, and a new dark age. And of course, in that context, it is the merger of business and the state which is central – which, as Mussolini said, is corporatism, or what he said is the proper term for fascism. This is the central context, and anyone who does not see it yet must be living under a rock.

We are facing corporate fascism – on a global scale. And people are talking about where to place the deck chairs for the best view.

Well, I have news for you: if we don't stop this trend, our view will be from under the heel of a jackboot.

*

If Britain had someone like Jeremy Corbyn as Prime Minister, or Tony Benn, then some serious economic stimulus and economic recovery could become a real possibility, and a reality, along with a recovery of sovereignty, democracy, and freedom from virtual serfdom under the neo-feudal banking cartel. But instead, Britain has had forty years of the tweedle-dee and tweedle-dum of neoconservatism and neoliberalism, which are two sides of the same coin of corporate rule: and that is why the economy, like the democratic process, is shattered, and in dust and ruin.

Britain, like the US and Canada, has for the past 40 years gone head-long into a corporate-style globalization, where manufacturing, production, and profits, are off-shored, and shipped to China and other low-wage nations, along with Swiss bank accounts, Panama and the Cayman Islands, for the sake of higher corporate margins and yields, and greater wealth for the elite who control them. The results have been predictable: de-industrialization, massive unemployment, the destruction of the middle class, soaring poverty and inequality, and the general "third-worldization" of the formerly wealthy Western nations, as Noam Chomsky called it, presciently, more than a quarter century ago.

(I am an audiophile – I love music. And I love Britain's Cambridge Audio and Warfedale sound systems. But while both are still designed in Britain, both, I believe, are now manufactured, like almost everything else, in China. Meanwhile, Paradigm and Anthem, two Canadian audio companies, also with beautiful, high-quality systems, have decided to design *and craft* their sound systems in Canada – thus ensuring high quality, as well as good jobs at home. It *can* be done. But the business elite want maximum profit, regardless of the cost to the people, the planet, jobs or the environment – so globalization and offshoring to China is the norm. But this can change – *if* we want it.)

In other words, it is the feeding frenzy of the business elite, and the policies enacted by their political prostitutes, from Pinochet, Thatcher and Reagan, through to the present, which have wreaked economic devastation on Britain and the rest of the world. (See Naomi Klein,

The Shock Doctrine.) Blaming Brexit for such structural and systemic problems is utterly foolish, or else utterly deceitful.

*

The greatest danger facing the world today is the Western power elite – namely, the banking elite, the other corporate elites of the Global 500, and the Western political elite in the US, the EU and Canada, among other nations, who loyally serve their corporate masters. They are at war with democracy, civil liberties, freedom, constitutional rule, international law, the overwhelming majority of the people, and the Earth itself.

Not only that, but the war on democracy, the people and the Earth, which is escalating daily to ever greater levels, and which is global, not only threatens to destroy and eliminate all remnants of democracy, sovereignty, civil liberties and freedom, along with justice and equality; and is not only driving us towards a dark age of neo-feudalism, and to the total destruction of any decent future for humankind on Earth, due to severe and growing ecological malfeasance and environmental pillaging: but furthermore, the same rabidly anti-democratic elite are pushing us ever closer to world war, and to nuclear holocaust.

Has anyone noticed the war drums beating, while the encircling of Russia and China comes to completion; and the propaganda war heats up, in advance of a *hot* war? To say that this is extraordinarily dangerous is to make the gravest of understatements.

In this context, to pander to paranoia on lesser issues, almost trivial issues by comparison, or at least, comparatively minor issues, such as whether or not Britain leaves or remains in the EU, is not only foolish in the extreme, but positively delusional – that, or it is simple propaganda.

On these facts we should be perfectly clear.

Stay or go as you choose, Britain. But do choose democracy, choose freedom, choose independence: and choose justice, ecological soundness, and peace – or the rest is meaningless, and moot.

Let's start by dealing with the real world, and the central issues of our reality at this time: such as war and peace, the growing ecological crisis, justice and equality – and the question of whether we will live in a corporate plutocracy, in a new feudal era, or in free and democratic societies.

Brexit, in that context, is a relatively minor question. It is important, but it is dwarfed by larger, deeper issues, which urgently need to be addressed.

*

The European Union could potentially be a democratic institution, a tool of democracy and freedom for the people. But that would require a number of major and fundamental changes, such as the abolition of a common currency, controlled by a central European bank, and a strict decentralization of powers among member nations. At present, the EU has been thoroughly captured as an institution by the globally and regionally dominant business elite, and particularly the banking elite. I think you might have better luck at turning Cerberus into a tool of democracy, than the EU.

What would be more intelligent, and more readily feasible, would be to leave the EU, and to look towards the formation of federations and alliances among free and democratic sovereign nations. The European Union, as it now stands, is too controlled by the ECB and the banking elite to make it compatible with either freedom or democracy. For that reason, I say leaving might be best. But it is up to the people to decide – not the screaming pundits and hyperventilating chickens in the major media, but the people themselves.

*

Whatever our thoughts might be on Brexit, this much should be made clear. The entire question of whether Britain stays in the European Union or leaves, is a distraction. It has virtually nothing to do with the central issues of our time, for Britain, or for Europe, or for the world, whether or not the British people vote to stay in or leave the EU. The central issue and the central challenge of our time, for Britain, for Europe, for the Western world, and for the world as a whole, is whether the people will rule themselves, through some form of genuine participatory democracy, backed by constitutional law and a respect for both the environment and human rights, or whether we will continue, in Britain, in Europe, and across the West and around the world, to be ruled by bankers and business elites, while the middle class and the poor are plundered, and the Earth is looted and razed. This is the question of our time – not Brexit.

The house is burning down, and people are running around madly with garden sprinklers, watering the daisies. We must regain our perspective, or all truly *is* lost.

JTR,
July 13, 2016

Post-Script: Ralph Waldo Emerson once said, *"A foolish consistency is the hobgoblin of little minds."* And he was right. A stubborn refusal to change one's opinion or view based upon new information, is not a sign of strength of character, but of weakness of mind. In that light, I must say, I wrote this piece before hearing Yanis Varoufakis, Jeremy Corbyn and John Wight speak about the Brexit question. And I would say they make compelling arguments for staying in the EU. In short, I would now emphasize the central point I tried to make clear in this short essay: that the essential question is not whether Britain leaves or remains in the EU, but whether the people of Britain, and of Europe and the world, vigorously seek democracy, *which is under attack world-wide*, or whether they surrender to the slow-motion global coup that is rapidly devouring and destroying democracy world-wide? That is the central question, as I think I made quite clear. If the people decide to fight for democracy within the European Union, I fully support that choice. If they decide that an institution, an alliance, a trade block or a union that is ruled by Goldman Sachs and the European Central Bank is intolerable, then I can certainly sympathize with that as well. But the central question remains: do we fight for democracy, or do we let it die, and accept that the new, neoliberal and neoconservative corporate fascists have already won. You know my answer to that question.

The Canadian Deep State:
Big Money, Big Oil,
and
the Death of Democracy

*I*s the Oil Industry Canada's 'Deep State'? Of course it is – along with Bay Street, Wall Street, Langley and Washington, the City of London, Davos and Basel (which are, of course, the major centres of economic, "intelligence" or political police, political, and financial powers in the Western world).

Big Oil has ruled the US since at least 1961. (See Peter Dale Scott, *The American Deep State: Wall Street, Big Oil, and the Attack on US Democracy*.) And Big Oil has ruled Canada since Justin Trudeau's father, Pierre Trudeau, left the Prime Minister's office, nearly forty years ago.

That's why Canada is doing nothing of substance, and nothing at all serious, at the federal level to fight climate change; why our greenhouse gas emissions continue to rise; why we continue to fail at every promised climate change target; why the oil industry continues to be subsidized and given enormous tax breaks; the Tar Sands continue to be expanded, and Trudeau Junior continues to approve pipelines, and continues to treat the oil industry with ongoing servitude and kid gloves.

Canada is falling behind, primarily due to its loyalty to the fossil fuel industry, corporate powers, and Washington. The world is beginning to move rapidly toward a new, clean, renewable energy infrastructure, while Canada has tied itself, foolishly, to yesterday's dying, and deadly, technology – as well as to the sinking ship of the American Empire. This is simply foolish, even from an economic perspective, and it is disastrous from an environmental perspective.

Given that climate change is costing billions of dollars of damage a year already, and given that the oil industry only accounts for 7% of the Canadian economy, catering to Big Oil doesn't even makes sense from a purely economic perspective. Why then, does Big Oil continue to effectively dictate Canadian federal policy? You can call it vested elite interests, or institutional capture, or a deep state, if you wish. I'd prefer to say it more directly. It's simple corruption.

We give away our oil and gas resources, like our water, lumber and other resources, virtually for free, with a fragment of the royalty fees other nations charge. Norway has the biggest sovereign trust fund in the world, thanks largely to its intelligent policy of charging more reasonable royalty fees for oil extraction by foreign corporations. Canada, meanwhile, behaves like a colonized third world nation, and asks, meekly, that corporations leave a nickel in the jar by the door as they leave, after siphoning off the nation's oil, water, forests and other resources.

The global fossil fuel industry has a yearly revenue of roughly one trillion dollars Canadian, or $761 billion USD. And it receives a further $5 trillion a year in subsidies, according to the IMF. Somebody is making hundreds of billions of dollars a year in fossil fuel profits – but it certainly isn't flowing to the Canadian people. Big Oil sets the policies for the Canadian federal government; full funding for social programs, health care, education, or protection for the environment, along with the Canadian people and democracy, be damned.

Pierre Trudeau was, in my mind, the last decent – far from perfect, but decent – Prime Minister Canada had. Justin Trudeau is not carrying out his father's legacy. Trudeau Junior is following in the tradition of a line of successive, frankly corrupt Prime Ministers, bootlickers all, who have sold out the country, the people, and the planet, to corporate interests in the oil patch, Bay Street, Wall Street and Davos.

Thank you, Junior.

Your trial awaits. The revolution, however, will not.

JTR,
February 16, 2018

Climate Change,
Class War,
and
The Continuing Assault
On Democracy and The Earth

~

Starring Justin Bieber Trudeau,
and
His Evil Twin,
The Boy Blunder of Washington

*R*ecently, Rolling Stone magazine published an issue with Justin Trudeau on the cover, asking, *"Why can't he be our president?"* Rolling Stone used to be known, at least to some degree, especially with Matt Taibbi, for having serious, thoughtful political commentary. But apparently Rolling Stoned queued up in the wrong line, and ended up with a lobotomy rather than a latte.

But in Canada, too, the starry-eyed day-dreaming also continues. We are supposed to love Justin Trudeau, or at the very least, be thrilled and eternally grateful that at least he isn't Stephen Harper, the widely reviled former Conservative Prime Minister; or worse, the boy blunder of Washington, the star of international buffoons, everybody's favourite sociopath and right-wing nut-case – you know who.... Mr. President Phrump.

But are they so very different in reality, as opposed to media presentation and image? As *Canadian Dimension* magazine pointed out, Trudeau Junior really isn't very different at all, in terms of policies, from Stephen, "The Bloodless" Harper. And Mr. Phrump isn't that far removed either – when viewed objectively, and the media hype is stripped away.

Trudeau (Junior) is a smiling fuzzy-bear cartoon liberal who likes to pose shirtless hiking in the woods for Facebook fans; presenting himself as a woodsy, folksy, earthy populist and friend of the people: when in fact, he is a servile and willing corporate peon. He looks good on the surface, but look a little deeper, and it is clear he would sell your grandmother for a nickel – and maybe his own as well.

Trump is a right-wing version of the false populism of Trudeau: less polished, more unstable, but not so very different. Trump also presents himself as a populist, and a friend of the people, but is likewise in service to the same ruling corporate elite, despite his pretense of being a rebel maverick and champion of the working man and woman.

Trump is a snake oil salesman who is enjoying his fifteen minutes of fame while he sells out the country to the robber barons on Wall Street who have ruled for generations. Trudeau is possibly more dangerous, precisely because he is so slick and polished, and far less obvious – but considering that both are active and eager, willing accomplices to the ongoing class war, and the rape and pillage of the middle class, the poor and the Earth by the super-rich billionaire elite, we would be foolish in the extreme to rally behind, or even passively support or tolerate, either one.

Both of these clowns in high places spell global neo-feudal corporate rule, and the end of sovereignty, freedom and democracy. Both spell the death of the middle class and the continuing growth of poverty and inequality. And both spell ecological holocaust, and the eradication of any viable or decent future for humankind. These are the facts, despite all the rhetoric and posturing, lip service, PR, and hot air.

In both cases, we've been duped, and sold a bill of goods. In both cases, it is business as usual, while the corporate elite continue their global plunder, poverty soars, the middle class is eviscerated, consumed and destroyed, and the Earth's ecosystem is pushed ever closer to collapse.

It is time for real change.

JTR,
August 19, 2017

What Is to Be Done?

*L*et's be clear from the start, and address the minority who are still held captive by Red Scare propaganda. Marxist-Leninism has been thoroughly discredited all over the world, including among the political activists of the world; and even if there was any hope of resurrecting it, we should not want to, because it was disastrously elitist and authoritarian, and it produced horrors that were worse than that of the Tzar, horrors they tried to solve. So, to any sensible, thoughtful person living in the 21st century, Marxist-Leninism is simply not an option. It is dead. Thank the Lord.

At the same time, we must acknowledge that liberal democracy has been destroyed, and is also dead.

We could say that there was a quiet, slow-motion coup, and the rising trans-national corporate elite took over the state; took over what was later-stage liberal democracy, which had become corrupted to the point of being crony capitalism, with the state serving the giants of capital, and transformed it, by swallowing it whole, into the merger of business and the state – which, of course, is what Mussolini described as corporatism, and said was the proper word for fascism.

And that is true. That is correct. That is just what transpired, between 1971, and especially 1979/80, when neoliberalism (and its mirror image of neoconservatism) seized two nation-state super-powers, with Thatcher and Reagan; and 2001-2008, when the Bush-Cheney cabal introduced the Patriot Act in 2001 and nullified the Constitution and Bill of Rights; then destroyed habeas corpus and 800 years of constitutional law stemming from the Magna Carta in 1215 with the Military Commissions

Act of 2006; created another wing of the new Gestapo (the established wings being the CIA, FBI and NSA, of course) with the Department of Homeland Security; and began the two-part process of transforming the US from a business-run liberal democracy into a corporatist oligarchy and police state. Obama then cemented the transformation from open democracy to police state and oligarchy, with his continued support of global surveillance, permanent war and militarization of the police; his signature to make central provisions of the Patriot Act permanent; his continuation of the Bush-Cheney Wall Street banker bailouts, the greatest transfer of wealth from Main Street to Wall Street in history, totalling nearly $20 trillion; lining his government with his banker friends who heavily funded his election; and finally, signing into effect full permanent immunity from any legal prosecution for the bankers who crashed the global economy in 2007-2008, thereby completing the consolidation of power which the ruling corporate power elite had sought, under the new crypto-fascist oligarchy of global corporate rule.

Or we could say that liberal democracy followed the natural course of its own evolution, either failing or refusing to see the inherent contradictions, which Jefferson saw, and Marx as well, which was always leading towards ever greater, increasing concentrations of wealth and economic power, leading inevitably to ever greater concentrations of social and political power, as is axiomatic and self-evident from history, until liberal democracy devoured itself, or was devoured by its own offspring, its own spawn, which is the transnational corporations, and more precisely, the transnational corporate elite: which is the less than 400 individuals who have become the Global Power Elite , who are now the de facto rulers of the world.

Liberal democracy was a deeply flawed system, not a golden age, as many who foolishly bemoan its loss may think. It gave us near-permanent war, imperialism, global pillage and destabilization, increasing risk of nuclear war, crony capitalism, self-insulating elites seeking their own glory, ego-gratification, and personal gain while pretending to be the servants and the friends, and the saviours, of the people; and it gave us the beginnings of the ecological holocaust, which we have created and set into motion, and which now heads towards us, like some great lumbering beast, come awake at last.

If corruption, creeping authoritarianism, bureaucracy, crony capitalism, imperialism, war, and systemic injustice make it impossible for us to wish to go back to liberal democracy, which is now dead – or should make it impossible for us to wish to go back to that; the environmental crisis makes it impossible to go back to liberal democracy under any conditions, because liberal democracy was radically out of balance and at odds with nature, at war with nature, apparent by its very ideological structure and quasi-religious program of *Growth or Death!* – which is really the motto of only one other entity on Earth, and that is cancer.

We need a new way, not the old ways. Marxist-Leninism is dead. Leftist authoritarianism has been thoroughly discredited world-wide and is a dead ideology. The ideology of "free market" capitalism, or neoliberalism – which really means discipline for the many, but freedom and state subsidies and a feeding trough for the elite – has lost its legitimacy around the world, and is about to join Maoism, Stalinism, Marxist-Leninism and the Ptolemaic world view, as a dead ideology.

The "Third Way" proposed by Tony Blair and others, never really took off as a powerful force, because the people could see from early on that it was a ruse, another fancy packaging of the same rotting formula of neoconservative/neoliberal snake oil, which makes trillions of dollars a year for the super-rich elite who sell it, and causes great suffering for the billions who are forced to swallow it – whether it be under the name of IMF Structural Adjustment Policies, austerity, slashing of social programs and environmental protection, or increasing rounds of obscenely lavish bailouts for the super-rich and their criminally run and floundering banks, or more billions and trillions for war and war preparations, while people go hungry, homeless, and without access to the education, health care or pensions they need.

I am not suggesting here a blueprint for a better society. That, I think, is too fraught with hubris to be safe, and I agree with Chomsky and other (left) libertarians on that. What I am proposing is that if we do not become a great deal more actively engaged in our world, in our reality, in our own lives, and in the shaping of our future, and great deal more bold, then we will have no future.

I am suggesting that if we do not have revolution now, or extremely soon, then it will be too late. The environmental crisis will have been neglected for too long – for that is what this newest of empires, which is the global neo-feudal, crypto-fascist corporate empire, is determined to do: neglect and avoid the crisis, and pay only lip service and make token gestures, feeling safely secure in their militarized luxury bunkers and remote retreats – and our civilization will start to crumble, then fall, from the impact and the weight of an ecological cataclysm that we were too slow to stop.

I am suggesting that we give democracy a real chance. But given that the corporate power-brokers have taken over the electoral process and the governments around the world, as well as the major media, and an increasing majority of the academy and the NGO sector, not to mention many of the churches, giving democracy a chance, by now, requires nothing short of revolution.

Democracy is dead. But not for long. In truth, it is an idea that cannot die. Therefore, it is only sleeping, like acorns under a frosty blanket of snow in winter, waiting for the spring rains to signal its time of new growth, and new beginnings.

Long live democracy! Long live freedom. This is not the end of history. This is, however, a new beginning.

*

Chomsky once summed things up extremely well. Actually, he seems to do that regularly. But I'm thinking of one specific remark made by the grand old gentleman of global dissidence. He said, *"You're either a democrat or an aristocrat."* That one short line sums up everything. Either you believe that the people should rule themselves – since that is what democracy means: *demos critos: people power* – or you believe in some form or another of elite rule.

Five thousand years of the rule of empires, of elite rule, have brought humanity to the brink of self-destruction. It is here that we correct our error and follow a new path – based in real democracy, with both constitutional and cultural protections for the rights and freedoms and dignity of all people and all individuals, based in a respect for the Earth and for all living creatures on Earth, based on the knowledge that we must be diverse by our nature, and out of a genuine respect for human freedom, and human dignity, and with the clear knowledge that we must also be united – or we simply perish from this Earth.

We will see a new democracy, under a new constitution, with a new mandate from the people, arisen from the streets; then, later, verified and confirmed in the ballot box – on hand-written ballots, counted by hand, and verified by international monitors, where election fraud is not permitted, and where private "donations" to elections are banned, and all elections are publicly funded.

We will reaffirm the rights and freedoms, and the dignity, of all people, of all individuals. We will overturn any and all fascist, or crypto-fascist, proto-fascist, or anti-democratic legislation, such as the Patriot Act and the NDAA, and strike down the disastrous mistake of the US Supreme Court in its foolish decision to misapply the 14ᵗʰ Amendment of the Constitution, which granted corporations the legal status and rights of persons.

We will abolish the US Electoral Colleges, which only impede, distort, and undermine democracy, and subvert the will of the people and the proper functioning of the people; and we will abolish the archaic "first-past-the-post" electoral system, which likewise undermines, thwarts and corrupts democracy. Both of these prevent genuine democracy from arising, and uphold, instead, vested interests and elite rule.

We will, perhaps above all, or at least, most urgently, democratize the media and the banks.

The banking elite have taken over. They have wildly destabilized the global economy. They are parasitically feeding off the global economy, while producing nothing of value, only a siphoning and a vampiric blood-draining; and they are now so powerful that they effectively control virtually every nation in the world.

We will, therefore, seize the assets of the banking elite and forensically audit their books, so that nothing is hidden. We will revoke and destroy their corporate charters and redistribute their net assets (some of them being zero, since they are being propped up by constant cash injections from governments to survive, but in total, likely amounting to trillions of dollars) among the people of the Earth, whom the banking elite have been pillaging for decades, centuries and generations.

*

As an aside, but an important one, I must remind people, if they haven't done so already: switch off the major media. Six corporations now control the world's major media, and what they produce, or more often, simply deliver, or distribute, is not "news" or "analysis," but simple propaganda, crafted by and for the benefit of, the ruling global power elite. This should come as no shock to anyone who is at all well-informed.

If there is any trace of doubt, watch the film, *Manufacturing Consent*, or read the book by Edward S. Herman and Noam Chomsky. And *everyone* who can read, who is over the age of fifteen, should consider a few books, at least, as absolutely required reading, including Chomsky's, *Necessary Illusions: Thought Control in Democratic Societies*.

These books should confirm the obvious: the major media function as propaganda tools for the ruling elite. Their "news" is a mixture of 80% propaganda, distortion, lies, half-truths, and spin, 10% truth, and 10% filler and fluff. And good luck discerning which is which. Unless you are heavily investing your time in references and resources that are far more honest and far more reliable than the major media, you will likely never know. Their "news" is far worse than unreliable, far worse than utterly unreliable: it is poison for your mind. Turn it off now.

And keep the other major sources of mental toxins, distraction, propaganda and fluff: television, "smart phones" and "social media," to a bare minimum as well. They're like refined sugar, or doughnuts: a little bit once in a while won't hurt you; but a steady diet will make you fat, sick, lethargic and dumb.

I'm serious. Refined sugar is rat poison. So is most of the content of television, cell phone chatter, and "social media," as more and more people are becoming aware. Turn it off. Unplug. Talk to another human being – face to face. Spend time alone in silent reflection. Tend your garden. Reconnect with nature, and with yourself. Get outside. Take care of your body; and nourish your body, your spirit, and also your mind. Watch a good film, or read a good book, or look for more honest and reliable journals as an alternative to major media.

I mention this, although it should be self-evident, at this moment as an interjection, because I glanced this morning at a headline from a major British newspaper, *The Independent*, which as usual, had nothing useful to say.

After many months of the major media regaling its readers with scare stories about the sky falling if Britain leaves Europe, the seemingly respectable Independent says something like, *Westminster and Brussels: How they can learn from one another.*

Really, this is the best the major media can offer? This is intelligent commentary?

Westminster, the British Parliament, is run by a band of frankly sociopathic criminal bankers from the City of London, as everyone who is paying attention at all knows very well. Brussels, the European Parliament, which the British people are rightly even more wary of than Westminster, is run by the European Central Bank and Goldman Sachs. And the best the major media can offer in their "analysis" of Britain, Europe, and the Brexit question, is that these two tightly interwoven bands of criminals can learn from one another?

How about addressing the profound and glaring deficit of democracy? But no, that kind of honest commentary can never appear in the major media "news" – because the major media are run by, and run for the benefit of – and owned or controlled, either directly, or through advertising dependency, or by being controlled by the governments and states which are in turn controlled by – the same global banking elite and other corporate elites, along with their political prostitute friends, who line the seats of Westminster and Brussels, along with Washington, Ottawa, Paris, Berlin, and most of the capitals of the world.

This is exactly what the great majority of people world-wide are beginning to suspect, and an increasing number know very well. I am simply telling people to trust their gut – they're right.

Henry David Thoreau, whom I love dearly and respect greatly, said, *"You should read the best books first; otherwise, you may never read them at all."* How true, and how wise, is that statement. And if there is no time for junk books, then there is certainly no time for junk "news." Turn it off.

(I have to say, after 30 years and fifty thousand hours of research, reading and reflection in politics, philosophy and world issues, I came to a point where I could no longer be immersed, virtually 24 hours a day, seven days a week, in serious, often heavy subjects. I was forced to acknowledge that I cannot continue to work as if life were a never-ending marathon, which I insisted upon sprinting. I had to accept that breaks are necessary, and that time for light reading, or light films, for sports and games and lounging on the beach, is simply necessary in order to continue on, without burning out or getting sick. I now try to live a more balanced life, and I strictly limit my daily and weekly doses of serious reading, viewing, or discussion. And my energy is improving, and my perspective, I believe, is more clear, as a result. So yes, there is time, and should be time, for lightness and relaxation, and simple fun, of course. I refuse to turn my back on humanity and the Earth. I refuse to accept the standard narrative without investigating things for myself. I still insist on doing my own homework, and thinking for myself, after serious reading and reflection. But sometimes, I just want to watch M*A*S*H, or Star Trek, SCTV or WKRP on DVD – or NHL playoffs, or football, or Father Ted...or a Kurt Russell, Clint Eastwood, Bruce Lee or Jet Li film; or read some light fiction (I love Terry Brooks novels). But nevertheless, and more than ever, I refuse to ingest poison, whether it is physical, or mental. I suggest others do the same.)

*

Along with the forced break-up and dissolution of the biggest banks and financial institutions and the redistribution of their assets to the people of the Earth – directly, or in locally held trusts (I would trust Oxfam to facilitate local trusts and their disbursements in the poorest communities and neighbourhoods on Earth, with multilateral monitoring that is open and transparent, to make everyone sure it is done properly, and then let the local people use their own councils and public meetings to decide what to do with the windfall), a global debt jubilee – an idea contained in the Bible, and brought to light and advocated recently by one of the world's leading financial analysts, Michael Hudson, which would be a writing down, a cancelling, of all personal and government debt – would change the world.

These two measures alone, would spell a renewal, a rebirth, and a new lease on life for people, for communities, and for nations, all around the world. And these two things we must, and will, simply do: because ethically they must be done; and because the people have been fed upon by blood-sucking, usurious, corporate banking vampires for long enough. It is time for the swindlers to pay back some of what they illegitimately acquired, and effectively stole.

*

In the US and other nations, anti-trust legislation exists – but is seldom used. The laws may have teeth, but the people do not. The laws have boldness, but the people have lacked all conviction, as Yeats wrote in his poem *"The Second Coming."* But that is about to change. Anti-trust laws must be invoked, and giant empires broken up – either dissolved completely, as in the case of merchants of death, such as the biotech industry, the chemical giants, the tobacco industry, and the arms industry, with their assets being liquidated and divided equally among the citizens of the world; or transformed, if possible, into dozens or hundreds of local democratic worker-run co-ops producing goods and services that do not kill, poison or destroy life, but support it.

The banking and media empires, along with the fossil fuel and arms industries, and the ecocidal biotech and chemical industries, must be first on the chopping block, to be dismantled, de-chartered, and broken up.

I outlined a partial accounting of the process for the break-up of the big banks above. Of course, sensible banking regulation, which was in place between FDR and the Clinton administration, until Clinton abolished it, must be re-installed – and without loopholes and watering down. It is our money or our life, in this case. If we let the bankers continue to rule, their short-sighted greed and power-lust will destroy us, and the planet we live on. The madness of the bankers must be stopped, just as with the madness of the military-industrial-complex and the war profiteers, the mad scientists and pseudo-scientists in the biotech and chemical industries, and the resource extraction industries, who don't know when to lift their heads from the trough, and are driving us into global ecological bankruptcy.

The media empires must be broken up if democracy, or freedom, are to live. The six corporations which now control the major media world-wide act as an echo chamber, as veteran investigative journalist John Pilger has said, for whatever narratives the elite want the people to hear. The world has grown deeply Orwellian, and it is the combination of the hyper-concentration of wealth and power, the merger of business and the state, and the merger of the major media with the new corporate state, which has made it so. If we do not want to live in a Brave New World of darkly Orwellian, nightmarish terrors of new norms, we had better address the near total take-over of the media by the corporate empire and the states which it controls.

The simplest, and the safest and most effective way to deal with this is to simply invoke anti-trust legislation, and to break up the media giants. Freeze their assets. Strip them of their corporate charters. Ban them from printing or airing another word. Shut them down completely. Then break up their empires into local and regional democratic media cooperatives. Journalists of skill and integrity will flock to the new global network of independent media cooperatives, and the media will be reborn – free, fierce, independent, and powerful. And democracy will stand a fighting chance – and will be reborn as well.

Break up the big banks; cancel all personal and government debts, as both the Bible and the world's best financial-economic analyst have urged; revoke the charters and dissolve the corporations that are committing routine crimes against humanity and the Earth of the most severe degree; break up the media empires, so that once more, the people can raise their voices and be heard, and not be drowned out by the great blaring propaganda and mass-distraction machine; and let democracy, and our world, be reborn.

End the $5 trillion a year subsidies to the fossil fuel industry, cut military spending at least in half, and direct well over $6 trillion a year towards building a clean, green, renewable energy and transportation infrastructure for the world. We have more than enough money, wealth and resources to do what needs to be done, to transform rapidly and in a very short time from a self-destructive, fossil fuel-addicted society, to a truly sustainable green energy society. And in the process of building this massive infrastructure project for the 21st century, we will be creating millions of good jobs, and creating a vibrant, thriving economy.

And if there is any question as to a shortage of funds to pay for the necessary transition from fossil fuels to a renewable energy infrastructure, we should remember, there is an estimated $20 trillion in secret off-shore bank accounts held by the super-rich, holding illegitimately gained wealth, which, considering this is humanity's darkest hour, and hour of greatest crisis, can and should be re-appropriated, and used to do battle with the only real enemies: ignorance, illusion, greed, hate, and the self-destructive habits we have acquired along the way, which we are in the process of breaking out of. Seize these accounts. Redistribute the funds to heal the Earth and to end poverty world-wide.

Invoke a global wealth tax, collectable by any level of government, should federal governments be too timid or too corrupt to do so, to be used to build solar and wind power systems, dig wells and ponds, plant trees and gardens, and to re-green, regenerate, and heal the Earth. If people are greedy, and want to be extremely rich, we can be a tolerant society. But there must be limits set on vanity and greed. No one "needs" more than $100 million in wealth. Everything beyond that is taxed at 100%, and redistributed to the poorest, and for the healing of the commons and the Earth.

And we must abolish the UN Security Council. No one dares say it, but it is a necessity, since the Security Council merely serves to give the US a veto over world affairs, and makes the US the de facto ruler of the world, which of course, to a very real and large extent, it is. It may now be an empty shell of a dying empire, but it is still powerful, and though it has been swallowed whole by the transnational, global corporate empire, giving the US dominance over the UN remains an extremely dangerous and foolish thing to do. The UN General Assembly must put forth a proposal immediately, to abolish the Security Council, and vote to make it happen. This is almost an aside, compared to defanging the banking and media empires, but it is still critically and vitally important to world peace, and to freedom and democracy and human rights and well-being, everywhere.

This is a partial list of a modest set of proposals to save ourselves from destroying ourselves, and to create, not a utopian world, but a better world for all.

These things would be a good start. Or rather, they *will be* a good start. And I can see, and feel, the Reverend Dr. Martin Luther King Jr., and others now gone on but still with us, smile, and heartily concur.

But first, we have to reclaim our democracy. The people have to reclaim their power. *We* have to reclaim our power. And now.

JTR,
October 8, 2019

www.ingramcontent.com/pod-product-compliance
Lightning Source LLC
Chambersburg PA
CBHW021526270326
41930CB00008B/1115